D0734284

THE FABLES
OF
ÆSOP

Book-of-the-Month Club
New York

LIST OF FABLES

THE FOX
AND THE GRAPES

A hungry Fox saw some clusters of ripe Grapes hanging from a trellised vine. She resorted to all her tricks to get at them, but she could not reach them and tired herself out. At last she turned away, muttering to herself, "Well, who cares? I'm sure the Grapes are sour anyway."

THE BOWMAN AND THE LION

A very skillful Bowman went up into the mountains to hunt. All the animals of the forest ran at his approach; only the Lion challenged him to fight. "Stop," said the Bowman to the Lion. "Here is my messenger, who has something to say to you," and then he let fly an arrow. The Lion, wounded in the side, rushed away in terror. When he met a Fox who chided him for lack of courage, the Lion replied, "If the man sends so fearful a messenger, what will be the power of the man himself?"

THE KITE AND THE PIGEONS

Some Pigeons, terrified by the appearance of a Kite, called upon the Hawk to defend them. He agreed at once. When they had admitted the Hawk into their coop, they found that he killed a larger number of them in one day than the Kite could injure in a whole year.

Avoid solutions that are worse than the problem.

THE FOX AND THE GOAT

A Fox fell into a deep well and could not get out. A Goat, overcome with thirst, came to the same well and, seeing the Fox, inquired if the water tasted good. Pretending to be merry, the Fox praised the water, saying it was beyond excellent, and encouraged him to

come down. The Goat, thinking only of his thirst, jumped in and drank, whereby the Fox informed him of the difficulty they were both in and suggested a plan for their common escape. "If," said the Fox, "you place your feet upon the wall and bend your head, I will run up your back and escape, and I will help you out afterwards." The Goat agreed; the Fox leapt upon his back and, steadying himself on the Goat's horns, reached the opening of the well, climbed out, and began to make off as fast as he could. Hearing the Goat's protests, the Fox turned around and cried, "You foolish old fellow! If you had as many brains in your head as you have hairs in your beard, you would never have gone down the well before you had thought of a way out."

Look before you leap.

THE WOLF AND THE CRANE

A Wolf, in great agony from a bone stuck in his throat, offered a Crane a large sum if she would venture her head down his gullet and remove the bone. When the Crane was successful and modestly asked about the promised compensation, the Wolf, grinning and showing his teeth, exclaimed, "Why, you ingrate— to ask for any other reward after having been permitted to pull your head in safety from the jaws of a Wolf!"

When helping the wicked, expect no gratitude and be thankful if you escape with your life.

☾

THE VAIN JACKDAW

A Jackdaw, as vain and conceited as a plain gray bird could be, picked up feathers that some Peacocks had dropped and stuck them among his own. Ignoring his old companions, he introduced himself to the flock of Peacocks. They were suspicious of the Jackdaw and, stripping him of the cast-off plumes, sent him on his way. The humiliated Jackdaw returned to his dreary companions as if nothing had happened. But his former friends, remembering the airs he had put on, refused to take him back. "Had you only been contented with what nature gave you," they said, "you would have escaped the punishment of your betters and banishment from your equals."

THE ANT AND THE GRASSHOPPER

An Ant was spending a frosty winter's day drying grain he had collected during the summertime. A Grasshopper, dying of hunger, passed by and earnestly begged for a little food. The Ant inquired of him, "Why did you not stock up on food during the summer?" He replied, "I had no time. I passed my days singing." The Ant then said in derision, "If you are foolish enough to sing all summer, you'll dance supperless to bed in winter."

THE BOY AND THE SCORPION

A Boy hunting for Locusts had caught a good number when he saw a Scorpion and, mistaking him for a Locust, reached out his hand. The Scorpion, ready to sting, said, "If you had only touched me, my friend, you would have lost not just me, but also all your Locusts!"

THE WIDOW AND HER HEN

A Widow owned a Hen that gave her one egg each day. She often thought to herself how she might obtain two eggs daily instead of one, and at last decided to give her Hen a double portion of barley. From that day on the Hen became fat and sleek and never laid another egg.

Covetousness overtakes itself.

THE MOUNTAIN IN LABOR

A mighty rumbling was once heard within a Mountain. Crowds of people came from all over and watched for days. While the hordes assembled, conjecturing that some magnificent event would soon occur, out of the Mountain came a Mouse.

Don't make much ado about nothing.

THE COCK AND THE JEWEL

A Cock was scratching up the straw in a farmyard, searching for food for the Hens, when he came across a precious stone that by chance had found its way there. "Well," he said, "you are a very fine thing, no doubt, but right now give me a barleycorn before all the jewels in the world."

The Cock was sensible, but there are many silly people who don't recognize just what is of value to them. You can't eat a jewel.

THE KID AND THE WOLF

A Kid standing on the roof of a house saw a Wolf passing by and began to taunt and abuse him. The Wolf, looking up, said, "Coward! I hear you. Yet it is not you who mock me but the roof on which you stand."

Time and place often give the advantage to the weak over the strong.

THE EAGLE
AND THE FOX

An Eagle and a Fox became close friends and decided to share a home. The Eagle built her nest in the uppermost branches of a tall tree, while the Fox crept into a hole at its foot, where she raised her young. Not long after, the Eagle, needing food for her own offspring, swooped down, seized one of the Fox's cubs, and carried it back to her nest. The Eagle did not fear retribution because of her lofty dwelling, but the Fox snatched a torch from a nearby altar and set the tree on fire. The helpless Eaglets were roasted in their nest and fell down dead at the bottom of the tree, where the Fox gobbled them up in sight of their mother.

The tyrant may not fear the tears of the oppressed, but he is never safe from their vengeance.

THE FAWN AND HER MOTHER

A young Fawn once said to her Mother, "You are larger than a dog, and swifter, and better winded, and you have horns as a defense. Why, then, are you always so afraid of the hounds?" The Mother smiled and said, "I know full well, my child, that what you say is true. I have the advantages you mention, but no sooner do I hear a dog bark than I feel faint and run off as fast as I can."

No arguments will give courage to the coward.

THE FOX AND THE LION

A Fox who had never seen a Lion fell in with one by chance for the first time and was so scared that he nearly died of fright. On seeing him a second time, he was still afraid, but not as badly as before. On the third meeting, the Fox felt so empowered that he went up to the Lion and engaged him in small talk.

Acquaintance softens prejudices. Familiarity breeds contempt.

THE OLD HOUND

A Hound who had been excellent in his youth became worn out with the weight of years and injuries. One day, while hunting a Wild Boar, he seized the creature's ear but could not hold on because of the decline of his teeth. The Boar escaped and the Hound's master was very disappointed. As the man was berating the Hound, the dog looked up and said, "Spare me. It was my power, not my will, that failed. Remember what I was, rather than abuse me for what I am."

THE HORSE AND THE GROOM

A Groom spent whole days grooming and rubbing down his Horse but sold the animal's feed for his own profit. "Alas!" said the Horse one day, "if you really wish me to look good, you should groom me less and feed me more."

THE FIGHTING COCKS
AND THE EAGLE

Two Game Cocks were fiercely fighting for the rule of the farmyard. At last the losing Crow crept into a corner of the hen house to lick his wounds. The conqueror flew up to a high wall, flapping his wings and crowing exultantly. An Eagle sailing through the air pounced upon him and carried him off in his claws. The defeated Crow then came out of his corner and henceforth ruled with undisputed mastery.

Pride before destruction.

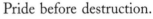

THE TWO BAGS

According to an ancient legend, every man is born into the world with two bags suspended from his neck—a small bag kept in front, full of his neighbors' faults, and a large bag held behind, filled with his own. Hence it is that men are quick to see the faults of others and yet are often blind to their own more numerous failings.

THE COUNTRYMAN
AND THE SNAKE

A Countryman, returning home one winter's day, found a Snake by some trees, half-dead from the cold. Taking pity on the creature, he placed it inside his cloak and brought it home to warm up by the fire. The Snake quickly thawed, then attacked the man and his children. Upon this the Countryman picked up an axe and killed the Snake.

Those who repay good with evil may expect their neighbor's pity to wear out.

THE FISHERMAN PIPING

A Fisherman who liked music more than his vocation took his flute and his nets to the seashore. Standing on an overhanging rock, he played several tunes in the hope that the fish, attracted by his melody, would dance into the net placed below. After playing a long time without being rewarded, he laid aside his flute and, casting his net into the sea, caught a great multitude of fish. When he saw them flapping about in the net, he smiled and said, "When I piped you would not dance, so I will have none of your dancing now."

It is great art to do the right thing at the right time.

THE MAN AND THE SATYR

A Man and a Satyr once sat down to eat on a very cold day. As they talked, the Man put his fingers to his mouth and blew on them. The Satyr inquired the

reason for this and was told that it was to warm the Man's hands. Later, as hot food was set before them, the Man raised one of the dishes towards his mouth and blew on his porridge. When the Satyr again inquired the reason for this, the Man said that he did it to cool the soup. "I can no longer consider you a friend," said the Satyr, "for I will have nothing to do with a man who blows hot and cold with the same mouth."

THE DOG AND THE SHADOW

A Dog who stole a piece of meat from a butcher's shop was crossing a river on his way home when he saw his Shadow reflected in the stream below. Thinking it was another dog with a piece of meat, he decided to steal that meat also; but in reaching for the treasure he dropped the piece he was carrying and so lost all.

Grasp at the shadow and lose the substance.

THE LION AND THE FOX

A Fox agreed to become a Lion's servant. Each performed his part, the Fox pointing out the prey and the Lion seizing it. The Fox, now jealous, began to think himself as good as his master and begged to be allowed to capture the prey, as well. The Lion agreed, but the next day, while attempting to snatch a lamb from a fold, the Fox was captured by a huntsman.

Keep to your place and your place will keep you.

JUPITER AND THE CAMEL

The Camel, jealous of the Bull's horns, asked Jupiter to bestow upon him the same appendages. Jupiter not only refused to give him the horns, he cropped his ears short for his impertinence.

By asking too much we may lose the little we have.

THE ASS AND THE GRASSHOPPERS

An Ass, hearing some Grasshoppers chirping, was delighted with their music and asked them what they ate to make them sing so sweetly. When they answered that they supped on nothing but dew, the Ass took up the same diet and soon died of hunger.

One man's meat is another man's poison.

THE WOLF AND THE LAMB

As a Wolf was drinking from a running brook, he spied a stray Lamb paddling at some distance down the stream. He decided to eat the Lamb but wondered to himself how he could justify his violence. "Villain!" said he, running up to the Lamb, "how dare you churn up the water I am drinking?" "I do not see how I can disturb the water, since it runs from you to me, not from me to you." "Well, then," replied the Wolf, "a year ago you called me names." "Sir," said the

Lamb, now frightened, "a year ago I was not born." "Well," replied the Wolf, "it must have been your father. Don't try to argue me out of my supper," and he gobbled up the Lamb.

The tyrant will always find a reason for his tyranny.

☾

THE FLIES AND THE HONEY POT

After a jar of honey was upset in a housekeeper's room, a number of Flies were attracted by its sweetness and ate greedily. Their feet, however, became so smeared with the honey that they could not release themselves and were suffocated. Just as they were dying, they exclaimed, "Oh, we are foolish creatures—for the sake of a little pleasure we have thrown away our lives!"

Pleasure sometimes brings pain.

℮

THE CREAKING WHEELS

A heavy wagon was being dragged along a country lane by a team of Oxen. The Wheels groaned and creaked terribly, until the Oxen turned around and said, "Hey! Why so much noise? We do all the work; it is we, not you, who ought to cry out."

Those who cry the loudest are not always the most hurt.

THE COUNTRY MOUSE
AND THE TOWN MOUSE

A Country Mouse invited a Town Mouse, an old friend, to pay him a visit and partake of his country life. As they ate their wheat stalks and roots pulled up from the hedges, the Town Mouse said to his friend, "How can you eat such dull food? In my house I am surrounded with every luxury; if you come with me, you can share my gourmet fare." The Country Mouse of course agreed and returned to town with his friend. On their arrival the Town Mouse placed before the Country Mouse bread, barley, beans, dried figs, honey, raisins, and, last of all, a tasty piece of cheese. Much delighted at the sight of such good cheer, the Country Mouse expressed his satisfaction and bemoaned his own dreary life. But just as they were beginning to eat, someone opened the kitchen door, and they both ran off as fast as they could to a hole so narrow that two could only find room in it by squeezing. They had scarcely returned to their feast when someone else entered the room, to take something out of a cupboard, and the two mice, more frightened than before, ran away and hid themselves again. At last the Country Mouse, now famished, said to his friend, "Although you've promised me a delicious feast, I'm leaving you to enjoy it yourself. It is surrounded by too many dangers. I'd rather have my wheat stalks and roots and eat in peace."

THE LION AND THE MOUSE

A Lion was awakened one night by a Mouse running across his face. Furious, the Lion caught the Mouse and was about to kill him when the tiny

creature pleaded, "If you would only spare my life, I would be sure to repay your kindness." The Lion, feeling generous, let him go with a laugh. Shortly after this the Lion was caught by some hunters, who tied him up with strong ropes. The Mouse, recognizing his benefactor's roar, came up and gnawed through the rope with his teeth, setting the Lion free. The Mouse then said, "You ridiculed the idea of my ever being able to help you, but now you know that it is possible for even a Mouse to come to the aid of a Lion."

THE DOG, THE COCK, AND THE FOX

A Dog and a Cock, having struck up a friendship, went out on their travels together. At nightfall they took shelter in a thick forest. The Cock perched himself on the branches of a tree, while the Dog found a bed on the ground within the hollow trunk. When morning dawned, the Cock, in his usual manner, crowed very loudly several times. A nearby Fox heard the sound and, wishing to feast on the Cock for breakfast, came and stood under the branches, saying how earnestly he desired to meet the owner of so magnificent a voice. The Cock, suspicious of the Fox's civilities, said, "Sir, go round to the hollow trunk below me and wake up the porter. He will let you in." On the Fox's approach, the Dog sprung out, caught him, and tore him to pieces.

Those who lay traps for others often are caught by their own bait.

THE SICK STAG

A Stag fell sick and lay down in a quiet corner of its pasture. His companions came in great numbers to inquire after his health, each one helping himself to some grass. Eventually the Stag recovered from his illness, but, as all his grass had been gobbled up by his friends, he died of starvation.

With friends like this, who needs enemies?

THE HARE AND THE TORTOISE

A Hare one day jeered at the slow pace of a Tortoise. The latter, laughing said, "Though you are as swift as the wind, I'm sure I could beat you in a race." The Hare, finding the proposal impossible, immediately assented. On the day of the race the Hare and the Tortoise started together. The Tortoise moved with a slow but steady pace; the Hare, trusting his own swiftness, cared little about the race and, lying down by the road, fell fast asleep. The Tortoise plodded on, but the Hare overslept and awoke to find the Tortoise crossing the finish line.

Slow and steady wins the race.

THE HOUSE DOG AND THE WOLF

A lean, hungry Wolf one night met a plump, well-fed House Dog. "How is it, my friend," said the Wolf, "that you look so sleek? How well your food agrees with you! Here I am struggling each day and can hardly save myself from starving." "Well," said the Dog, "all I have to do is guard the master's house from thieves." "Sounds like a good deal," said the Wolf. "Yes," said the Dog, "you have nothing to lose. Come along with me and I'll set you up." Along the way the Wolf spied a curious mark on the Dog's neck and inquired about it. "Oh, it's nothing," said the Dog, "only the place where a chain is attached to my collar." "Chain!" cried the Wolf in surprise. "You mean you can't roam free?" "Well, some people are afraid of me, so I'm tied up during the day. But I assure you, I have perfect liberty at night, plus the master feeds me from his own plate, the servants give me their leftovers, and everyone is so kind to me—but, where are you going?" "You can have this job," said the Wolf. "I'll take a dry crust with freedom over a king's luxury with a chain any day."

THE OLD WOMAN
AND THE WINE JAR

An Old Woman found an empty cask that had once contained a fine old wine and that still retained the fragrant smell of its former contents. She greedily placed it several times under her nose and, drawing it backwards and forwards, said, "Delicious! How nice the Wine must have been when it leaves behind so sweet a perfume?"

The memory of a good deed lives on.

THE OX AND THE FROG

An Ox drinking at a pool trod on a brood of young Frogs, crushing one of them to death. The Mother came up and, noticing one of her sons missing, asked his brothers what had become of him. "He is dead, " said one of the Frogs. "Just now a huge beast with four big feet came to the pool and crushed him." The Mother Frog, puffing herself out, inquired, "Big? He can't be bigger than I." "Don't bother to puff yourself out, Mother," said her son. "Even if you were to burst yourself, you wouldn't be a fraction of his size."

Men are ruined by attempting a greatness at which they have no chance.

~❧~

THE CROW AND THE PITCHER

A Crow, dying of thirst, saw a Pitcher and, hoping to find water, flew to it with great delight. When he reached the urn, he discovered that it contained so little water that he could not possibly get at the liquid. He tried to break the Pitcher and to upset it, but all his efforts were in vain. At last he collected as many pebbles as he could carry and dropped them one by one with his beak into the Pitcher, raising the water to the brim and saving his life.

Necessity is the mother of invention.

THE TORTOISE AND THE EAGLE

A Tortoise, basking lazily in the sun, complained to the sea-birds how hard her life was because she could not fly. An Eagle hovering nearby heard her grumbling and asked what reward she would give if he would take her aloft and float her in the air. "I will give you," the Tortoise said, "all the riches of the Red Sea." "Then I will teach you to fly," said the Eagle; and, taking the Tortoise up in his claws, he carried her almost to the clouds. Suddenly he cried, "Now, then," and let her go, and the Tortoise fell onto a rock, smashing her shell to pieces.

Pride shall have a fall.

THE MULE

A Mule, silly from lack of work and too much corn, was showing off. He galloped about in a very extravagant manner, saying, "My mother was a high-minded racer, and I am her child in speed and spirit." The next day, being driven on a long journey and feeling very tired, the Mule exclaimed in a disconsolate tone, "Well my father, after all, was only an ass."

Every truth has two sides; it is best to look at both before committing oneself to either.

THE CRAB AND ITS MOTHER

A Crab one day said to her son, "Why do you walk so crooked? It is far better to go straight." The young Crab replied, "Quite true, Mother; why don't you show me how?"

Example is more powerful than reproach.

THE BOY WHO CRIED WOLF

A Shepherd Boy, tending his flock not far from a village, liked to amuse himself by crying out "Wolf! Wolf!" His trick succeeded two or three times; the whole village came running to his assistance, only to be laughed at for falling for his ruse. Then, one day, the Wolf came for real. The boy cried out in earnest, but his neighbors, thinking he was at his old sport, ignored his cries, and the Wolf devoured the sheep.

Liars are not believed, even when they tell the truth.

THE HEN AND THE CAT

A Cat, hearing that a Hen was laid up sick in her nest, paid her a visit, asking, "How are you, my dear friend? What can I do for you? What are you in want of? Is there is anything in the world I can bring you? Keep up your spirits and don't be alarmed." "Thank you," said the Hen. "If you'll be good enough to leave, I'm sure I'll soon be well."

Uninvited guests are often more welcome when they are gone.

THE FOX AND THE WOOD CUTTER

A Fox running from some hounds came across a Wood Cutter felling an oak and begged the man to show him a safe hiding place. The Wood Cutter advised him to take shelter in the Wood Cutter's own hut. A few minutes later the Huntsman came up with his hounds and asked the Wood Cutter if he had seen the Fox. He declared that he had not, but he pointed

to the hut where the Fox hid. The Huntsman, however, took no notice of the hint and, believing the Wood Cutter's word, went forward on his chase. As soon as the hunter was out of sight, the Fox departed the hut without saying a word, and the Wood Cutter called after him. "You ungrateful fellow," he cried, "you owe your life to me, and yet you leave without a word of thanks." The Fox replied, "I would thank you fervently if your deeds were as good as your words, and if your hands were not traitors to your speech."

There can be as much malice in a wink as in a word.

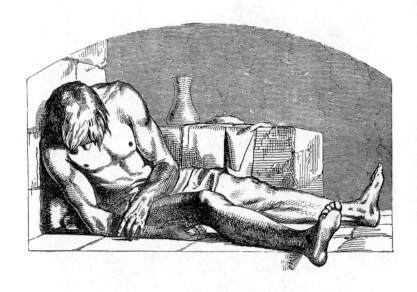

THE BELLY
AND ITS FELLOW BODY PARTS

The other Body Parts rebelled against the Belly, saying, "Why should we be always engaged in admin-
istering to your wants while you do nothing but take
your rest and enjoy yourself?" They carried out their
resolve and refused to assist the Belly, whereby the
whole body quickly became debilitated. The others
were then convinced that the Belly, as cumbersome and
useless as it seemed, had an important function, and
that they could no more do without it than it could do
without them.

THE BEAR AND THE
TWO TRAVELLERS

Two friends were travelling togeth-er when they suddenly met up with a Bear. One man quickly climbed a tree, hiding himself among the branches. The other, seeing that he had no chance of escape, fell flat on the ground, and when the Bear came up and felt the man with his snout, he held his breath and pretended to be dead. The Bear soon left, believing his ruse. When the beast was out of sight, the other man descended from the tree and jokingly asked his friend, "What was it the Bear whispered in your ear?" "Well," the man replied, "he gave me some advice: be careful of friends who leave you in the lurch."

Misfortune tests the sincerity of affection.

THE LION, THE FOX, AND THE ASS

The Lion, the Fox, and the Ass formed a party to go hunting. After a successful hunt the three celebrated over a hearty meal. The Lion asked the Ass to divide up the booty. The Ass divided the ·proceeds into three equal parts and asked his friends to choose their portions. The Lion, in great indignation, tore the Ass to pieces. He then asked the Fox to divide the booty. The Fox gathered almost everything into one pile, leaving only a tiny bit for himself. "Oh, friend," said the Lion, "who taught you to make so equitable a division?"

Happy is the man who learns from the misfortunes of others.

THE STAG IN THE OX STALL

A Stag, being hunted by hounds and distracted by fear, took shelter at the first farmhouse he saw, hiding himself in a shed with some Oxen. An ox kindly

said, "Oh, you poor creature! Why choose destruction by trusting yourself in the house of your enemy?" The Stag replied, "If you don't betray me, I'll be off at the first opportunity." As evening approached the herdsman came to feed the cattle but did not see the Stag, and later the estate manager came through with several laborers and failed to notice him. The Stag, now feeling secure, began to thank the Oxen who had helped him hide. One of them answered, "We do wish you well, but the danger is not yet over. There is one more person to pass through the shed, and until he has come and gone your life is still in peril." At that moment the master, having finished his supper, came by the shed to see that all was safe for the night. Approaching the racks, he cried out, "Why is there hardly any food? And why is there not enough straw? Those lazy fellows have not even swept the cobwebs away." While examining everything in turn, he spied the tips of the Stag's antlers peeping out of the straw. Summoning his servants, he ordered that the Stag be seized and killed.

There is no eye like the master's eye.

THE HARE AND THE HOUND

A Hound chasing a Hare gave up after a long while. A Goatherd, who was watching, mocked the dog, saying the Hare was a better runner. "You don't see the difference," replied the Hound. "I was only running for my dinner. He was running for his life."

THE DOLPHINS, THE WHALES, AND THE SPRAT

The Dolphins and Whales were waging a fierce war. While the battle was at its height, a Sprat lifted its head out of the waves and tried to mediate. But one of the Dolphins exclaimed, "Leave us alone! We'd rather perish than be reconciled by you."

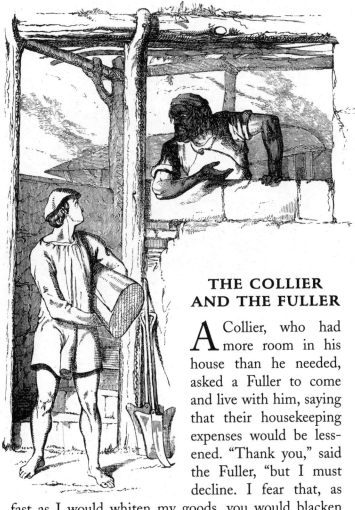

THE COLLIER AND THE FULLER

A Collier, who had more room in his house than he needed, asked a Fuller to come and live with him, saying that their housekeeping expenses would be lessened. "Thank you," said the Fuller, "but I must decline. I fear that, as fast as I would whiten my goods, you would blacken them again."

Like will draw like.

THE LION IN LOVE

A Lion demanded the daughter of a Wood Cutter in marriage. The father, unwilling to grant the request but afraid to refuse, decided on a plan. He expressed his willingness to accept the Lion as the suitor of his daughter if the beast would allow the man to extract his teeth and cut off his claws, as the daughter was afraid of both. The Lion cheerfully assented to the proposal and, returning with teeth and claws gone, he called upon the father to accept him as a son-in-law. The Wood Cutter, no longer afraid, set upon the Lion with a club and drove him away into the forest.

THE NORTH WIND AND THE SUN

A dispute once arose between the North Wind and the Sun over who was stronger, and they agreed that whoever could first make a Traveller remove his coat should be declared the victor. The North Wind tried first and blew with all his might; but the stronger he blew, the closer the Traveller wrapped his cloak around him. At last the North Wind called upon the Sun to see what he could do. The Sun broke out of the clouds and dispersed the cold and wind, and the Traveller, feeling the genial warmth as the Sun became hotter and hotter, sat down and cast his coat upon the ground.

Persuasion is better than force. The sunshine of a kind and gentle manner will sooner lay open a poor man's heart than all the threats of blustering authority.

THE FARMER AND HIS SONS

A Farmer who was close to death wanted to share his knowledge with his sons on the best way to keep up the farm. He called them to his bedside and said, "My children, all that I have to leave you can be found in the vineyards." The sons, thinking their father was referring to a hidden treasure, set to work with their spades and ploughs and overturned the soil again and again. They found no treasure, but the vines, strengthened by the thorough tillage, repaid their labor with an extraordinarily abundant crop.

Industry in itself is a treasure.

THE TREES AND THE AXE

A Woodman came into a forest and asked the Trees to provide him a handle for his Axe. The Trees agreed to the modest request and called upon a humble ash to furnish the wood. No sooner had the man fitted the new handle to his Axe than he began to use it with a vengeance, felling the noblest trees of the wood. An old oak, lamenting the destruction of his companions, whispered to a cedar, "Our concession is a disaster. If we had not given up our simple ash, we might have stood for ages."

When the rich surrender the rights of the poor, they give up a weapon to be used against their own privileges.

THE ONE-EYED DOE

A Doe, blind in one eye, used to graze near the sea. She turned her good eye towards the land, to keep watch on approaching hunters or hounds, and her bad eye towards the sea, where she thought there was no danger. But some boatmen sailing by saw her and, taking aim, mortally wounded her. With her last breath the Doe gasped, "How stupid to take such precautions against the land, only to find the sea much more perilous."

Troubles often come from the place where we least expect them.

THE ASS
AND THE LAP-DOG

An Ass and a Lap-dog belonged to the same master. The Ass was kept in the stable with plenty of corn and hay to eat, which was a fine life for an Ass. The Lap-dog, a great beauty, knew many tricks and fawned over his master, who allowed the dog to sit on his lap and spoiled him with special tidbits. The Ass had much work to do, carrying wood all day and grinding corn at night, and it galled him to see the Lap-dog live in such luxury. Deciding to court the master in the same way, he one day galloped into the master's house swishing his tail and mimicking the frolics of the favored dog. But he upset the table where the master was eating his dinner, breaking it in two and smashing all the dishes. Still trying to please, the Ass licked the master and jumped upon his back. The servants, perceiving the master to be in danger, drove the Ass out with sticks and staves. Back in his stall the Ass lamented, "Why couldn't I have been satisfied with my position without attempting to be as playful as a mere puppy?"

THE BLIND MAN AND THE WHELP

A Blind Man could distinguish different animals by touching them with his hands. One day a baby wolf was brought to him, with a request that the Blind Man say what it was. He felt the creature and, being in doubt, said, "I do not know whether your father was a fox or a wolf, but I know that I would not trust you among a flock of sheep."

Evil tendencies are shown early in life.

THE WOLVES
AND THE SHEEP

The Wolves once sent a delegation to the Sheep, desiring that the two sides make peace. "Why," they said, "are we always waging this deadly strife? Those dogs are the cause; they are always barking and provoking us. If they weren't here, there would no longer be any problem between us." The silly Sheep listened and dismissed the dogs, and their flock, now without protectors, thus became an easier target for their enemy.

HERCULES
AND THE WAGONER

A Wagoner was carelessly driving his wagon along a country lane when one wheel sank deep into a rut. The driver did nothing but utter loud cries to Hercules to come and help him. Hercules appeared and told the Wagoner to put his shoulder to the wheel, reminding him that Heaven aided only those who first tried to help themselves.

THE FOX
WHO LOST HIS TAIL

A Fox caught in a trap escaped but lost his tail in the struggle. Feeling self-conscious about his deficiency, he tried to make the other foxes follow his example. He called a meeting and advised them to cut off their tails, saying, "You have no idea of the ease and comfort with which I now move about." Upon this, one of the oldest stepped forward and said, "I'm sure, my friend, if you had any chance of recovering your own tail, you wouldn't be advising us to lose ours."

THE OLD WOMAN
AND THE PHYSICIAN

An Old Woman who had become blind called in a Physician to heal her. She bargained with him in the presence of witnesses: if he should cure her blindness, he would receive from her a handsome sum; but if her infirmity remained, she would give him nothing. The Physician applied a salve to her eyes and, on every visit to her home, took something with him until he had stolen all her property. When she was healed, he demanded the promised payment. The Old Woman, now sighted, saw that all of her goods were missing and gave him nothing. The Physician insisted on his money and summoned her before a judge. The Old Woman, standing up in court, said, "What this man says is true—I promised to give him a fee if my sight was restored; but if I continued to be blind, I was to give him nothing. Now he declares I am cured, but I disagree. Before I became blind, I could see all sorts of furniture and goods in my house, but now I see none."

He who plays a trick must be able to take a joke.

THE HARES AND THE FROGS

The Hares, driven desperate by the perpetual alarm that their many enemies caused them, determined to put an end to themselves and their troubles by jumping into a deep lake. As they scampered off in unison to carry out their plan, the Frogs lying on the banks of the lake heard the noise of their feet and rushed helter-skelter to the deep water for safety. On seeing the rapid disappearance of the Frogs, one of the Hares cried out to his companions, "Our case is not so desperate yet; here are other creatures more fainthearted than ourselves."

Whatever your misery, there are some whose lot is worse than your own.

THE FARMER AND THE STORK

A Farmer fixed a net in his field to catch the Cranes who came to feed on his corn. When he went to examine the net, he found a Stork among the Cranes. "Spare me," cried the Stork. "I have eaten none of your corn. I am no Crane but a Stork, a bird of excellent character, and I honor and slave for my mother and father." The Farmer laughed and said, "Say what you will, but I have caught you with those who are destroying my crops, and you must suffer what they will suffer."

Bad company proves more than fair professions. Birds of a feather flock together.

THE ANGLER AND THE LITTLE FISH

A professional Angler once caught only a single Little Fish as the result of a whole day's labor. The Fish, panting convulsively, begged for his life. "Sir, what good can I be to you?" he said. "As small as I am, I would make a sorry meal. Spare my life and throw me back into the sea. I shall soon become a large fish, fit for the tables of the rich, and then you can catch me again and make a handsome profit." The Angler replied, "I would indeed be a very simple fellow if, for the chance of a greater but uncertain profit, I were to give up my present slighter gain."

A bird in the hand is worth two in the bush.

THE MONKEY AND THE CAMEL

At a great meeting of the beasts, the Monkey stood up to dance. Having entertained the assembly, he sat down amidst great applause. The Camel, envious of the praises bestowed on the Monkey, took a turn to dance for the others' amusement. He moved about in so absurd a manner that the beasts, in a fit of indignation, set upon him with clubs and drove him out of the ring.

Stretch your arm no further than your sleeve will reach.

THE MOLE AND HIS MOTHER

A Mole, blind from birth, once said to his Mother, "I am sure that I can see!" In the desire to prove his mistake, his Mother placed before him a lump of frankincense and asked what it was. The young Mole said, "It's a pebble." The Mother exclaimed, "Oh, my child, I am afraid that not only are you blind, you can't smell either."

Brag about a defect and betray another.

THE LIONESS

There was a great controversy among the beasts of the field as to which produced the greatest number of offspring at a birth. They rushed clamorously into the presence of the Lioness and demanded of her,

"How many sons have you had at a birth?" The Lioness laughed at them and said, "One, but that one is a lion."

The value is in the worth, not in the number. Quality before quantity.

THE BUNDLE OF STICKS

A Man who had a quarrelsome family thought to give his sons a practical illustration of the evils of disharmony. One day he told them to lay a pile of Sticks before him. When they had done so, he tied the Sticks into a bundle and laid it into the hands of each of them in succession, ordering them to break it into pieces. Each tried with all his strength but was not able. The Man then untied the bundle and gave them the Sticks separately, and they broke them easily. He then said, "My sons, if you are of one mind and unite to

assist each other, you will be like this bundle, uninjured by all the attempts of your enemies; but if you are divided among yourselves, you will be broken as easily as these Sticks."

United we stand, divided we fall.

THE MAN AND THE LION

A Man and a Lion were once travelling together through the forest, and soon each began to boast of his superior strength. As the dispute heated up, they passed a statue that showed a man strangling a lion. The Man pointed to it and said, "See! What more proof do you need?" The Lion replied, "This is your version of the story. If lions could erect statues, you would see twenty dead men under the paw of that lion."

Men are unreliable narrators of their own stories.

THE NURSE
AND THE WOLF

A hungry Wolf was prowling about in the morning in search of food. As he passed the door of a forest cottage, he heard a Nurse say to a crying Child, "Be quiet, or I will throw you out of the window and the Wolf will eat you." So the Wolf sat down all day waiting at the door. In the evening he heard the same Nurse, now fondling the Child, saying, "That's a good baby; if the Wolf comes, we'll beat him to death." The disappointed Wolf ran home muttering, "This is what happens when you believe people who say one thing and mean another."

THE HORSE AND THE STAG

A Horse had a whole meadow to himself until a Stag intruded into his domain and damaged the pasture. The Horse, anxious for revenge, asked a Man to help him punish the Stag. "Yes," said the Man. "Let me put a bit into your mouth and climb on your back, and we'll go off to get some weapons." The Horse consented and the Man mounted him; but instead of getting his revenge on the Stag, from that time forward the Horse was a slave to the Man.

Revenge is too dearly purchased if its price is liberty.

THE WOLF AND THE SHEEP

A Wolf, sorely wounded by dogs, lay recovering in his lair. Being in want of food, he asked a Sheep who was passing by to fetch some water from a nearby stream. "If you will bring me drink," he said, "I will find meat myself." "No doubt," said the Sheep. "If I should bring you the drink, you would make mince-meat of *me*."

Hypocritical speeches are easily seen through.

THE WIDOW AND THE SHEEP

A certain poor Widow had only one Sheep. At shearing time, wishing to make the most of the wool, she sheared her Sheep so closely that she cut his flesh. The Sheep, writhing in pain, said, "Why do you hurt me so, mistress? What weight can my blood add to the wool? If you want my flesh, bring the butcher, who will kill me in an instant; but if you want my fleece, send for the shearer, who will clip my wool without drawing blood."

The least outlay does not always bring the greatest gain.

THE TRAVELLER AND HIS DOG

A Traveller, preparing to set out on a journey, saw his Dog standing at the door stretching himself. He asked the Dog sharply, "Why do you stand there gaping? Everything is ready but you!" The Dog, wagging his tail, replied, "Oh, I am quite ready, master; in fact, *I* have been waiting for *you*."

The loiterer often attributes the delays he causes to his more active friends.

THE SWALLOW AND THE RAVEN

The Swallow and the Raven fought over who was the finer bird. The Raven put an end to the dispute by saying, "Your feathers may be very beautiful in the spring, but mine protect me against the winter."

Durability is better than show.

THE LAMP

A Lamp soaked with too much oil and flaring very high boasted that it gave more light than the sun. Suddenly a puff of wind arose and extinguished it. As its Owner lit the Lamp again, he said, "From now on be content to give your light in silence. The stars don't need to be relit."

THE HERDSMAN
AND THE LOST BULL

A Herdsman tending cows in a forest lost a Bull
from the fold. After a long and fruitless search he
made a vow that, if he could only discover the thief who
had stolen the Bull, he would offer a lamb in sacrifice
to Hermes, Pan, and all the nymphs of the forest and
the mountain. Not long afterwards, as he ascended a

small hill, he saw at its foot a Lion feeding on the very same Bull. When the Lion spotted him, the Herdsman lifted his eyes and hands to heaven and said, "Now that I know who robbed me, I would gladly give up the Bull to secure my own escape."

Were our ill-judged prayers always granted, many men would be ruined.

THE TRAVELLERS AND THE SYCAMORE

Two Travellers, worn out by the heat of the summer's sun, lay themselves down at noon under the wide-spreading branches of a Sycamore. As they rested under its shade, one of the Travellers said to the other, "What a singularly useless tree is the Sycamore! It bears no fruit and is not of the least service to man." The tree, interrupting him, said, "How dare you describe me as useless while you enjoy the comfort of my shade?"

Some men don't recognize their best blessings.

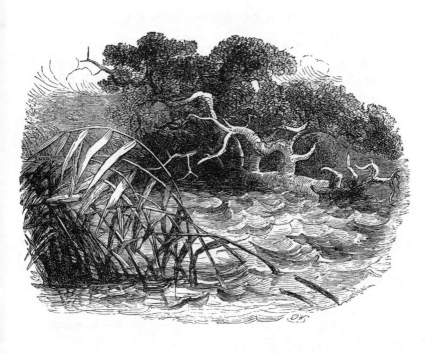

THE OAK AND THE REEDS

A very large Oak was uprooted by the wind and thrown across a stream. It fell among some Reeds, to whom it said, "I wonder how you who are so light and weak withstood the storm." They replied, "You fight the wind and are destroyed. We are saved by yielding and bending to the slightest breath."

Stoop to conquer.

THE MISCHIEVOUS DOG

There was a Dog so wild and mischievous that his master was forced to suspend a bell from his neck, so that all the neighbors would be warned of his presence. The Dog grew proud of his bell and ran through the marketplace with it jingling loudly. An old hound, fed up with the noise, said to him, "Why do you make such an exhibition of yourself? That bell is not a reward, but a mark of disgrace, a public notice to all to avoid you."

Notoriety is often mistaken for fame.

MERCURY
AND THE WOODMAN

A Woodman, felling trees by the side of a deep river, unintentionally dropped his axe into the water. As he sat on the bank lamenting his bad luck, Mercury appeared and asked the cause of his tears. After hearing the Woodman's tale Mercury dove into the river and brought up a golden axe. He inquired if it was the Woodman's, and the man said it was not. Mercury then disappeared beneath the water a second time and returned with a silver axe. Again he asked the

Woodman if this axe belonged to him, and the man said it did not. Mercury then dove into the pool for a third time and brought up the axe that had been lost. The Woodman claimed it and expressed his joy at its recovery, and, pleased with the man's honesty, Mercury gave him the golden and silver axes as well.

The Woodman returned home and related this story to his companions. One of them decided to see if he could secure the same good fortune for himself. He ran to the river, threw his axe into the water, and sat down on the bank to weep. Mercury appeared to him and, having learned the cause of his grief, plunged into the stream and brought up a golden axe. The man seized it greedily and declared that it was the very same axe that he had lost. Displeased at the man's knavery, Mercury not only took away the golden axe but refused to recover the one he had thrown into the river.

Honesty is the best policy.

THE GEESE AND THE CRANES

The Geese and Cranes fed together in the same meadow. One day a birdcatcher came to catch the birds with his nets. The Cranes, being light of body, flew off at his approach; but the Geese, weighed down by their fat, were captured.

In a pinch, those with the least baggage fare best.

THE LION AND
THE WILD ASS HUNTING

The Lion and the Wild Ass entered into an alliance with the intention of capturing the beasts of the forest with greater ease, the Lion contributing strength and the Wild Ass speed. When they had taken as many beasts as they needed, the Lion decided to distribute the prey, dividing it into three shares. "I will take the first part," he said, "because I am King. And the second I will take as a share in the chase. And the third—well, take it if you dare."

Might makes right.

JUPITER, NEPTUNE,
MINERVA, AND MOMUS

According to an ancient legend, the first man was made by Jupiter, the first bull by Neptune, and the first house by Minerva. On the completion of their labors, a dispute arose among them as to whose work was the most perfect. They agreed to appoint Momus as judge and to abide by his decision. Momus, however, was quite envious of the handicraft of each and found fault with their work. First Momus criticized Neptune because the god had not placed the horns of the bull below his eyes, so that the animal might better see where to strike. Momus then condemned the work of Jupiter because he had not placed the heart of man on the outside, so that everyone might read man's thoughts and feelings. And, lastly, he found fault with the house of Minerva because she had not built iron wheels into the foundation, so that inhabitants might easily move if a neighbor became unpleasant. Jupiter, indignant at such nit-picking, told Momus to refrain from criticizing others until he had created something himself, and he expelled Momus from Olympus.

☽

THE MARRIAGE OF THE SUN

Once upon a time, the Sun announced his intention to take a wife. All the birds and beasts were delighted at the thought, especially the frogs, who lifted up their voices to the sky. But one old toad put an end to the festivities by saying, "The Sun, now all alone, own, parches the marsh so that we can hardly bear it. What will be our future if he should have half a dozen little suns?"

THE THIEF AND HIS MOTHER

A Boy stole a lesson-book from one of his fellow students and took it home to his Mother. Instead of chastizing him for the theft, she encouraged him. Next he stole a cloak and brought it to her, and she further commended him. As the Boy grew older, he proceeded to steal things of greater value. At last he was caught and, with his hands bound behind him, was led away to the place of public execution. His Mother followed in the crowd and violently beat her breast in sorrow, whereupon the young man said, "I wish to say something to my Mother." She came close to him, and he quickly seized her ear with his teeth and bit it off. The Mother cried out loudly, calling him a monster, to which he replied, "If you had only beaten me when I first stole, I never would have come to this."

Nip evil in the bud.

THE CAT AND THE MICE

A Cat, grown feeble with age and no longer able to catch Mice, thought how she might entice them to come to her. Trying to pass herself off as a bag, or at least a dead cat, she suspended herself from a peg by her hind legs. An old mouse, who was smart enough to keep his distance, whispered to his friend, "I've seen lots of bags in my day, but never one with a cat's head." "Hang there as long as you like," said the other. "I wouldn't come near you even if you turned into a mealbag."

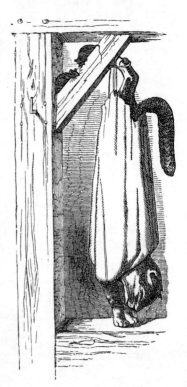

Old birds can't be lured with chaff.

THE LION AND
HIS THREE COUNCILLORS

The Lion called the Sheep to ask her if his breath smelled. She said yes, and he bit her head off for telling the truth. He called over the Wolf and asked the same question. The Wolf said no, and the Lion tore him to pieces for being a flatterer. At last he called the Fox and asked the question one more time. The Fox replied that he had a bad cold and could not smell.

The wise man says nothing in dangerous times.

THE MILK WOMAN AND HER PAIL

A farmer's daughter was carrying her Pail of milk from the field to the farmhouse when she started to daydream. "The money for this milk will buy at least three hundred eggs. The eggs, allowing for any mishaps, will produce two hundred and fifty chickens. The chickens will become ready for the market when poultry will fetch the highest price, so that by the end of the year I will have enough money to buy a new gown—green, because it goes with my complexion. In this dress I will go to the fair, where all the young fellows will propose to me, but I will toss my head and refuse them all." At that moment she tossed her head in unison with her thoughts and the milk Pail fell to the ground, putting an end to all her schemes.

THE OXEN AND THE BUTCHERS

The Oxen once sought to destroy the Butchers, whose art was their destruction. They assembled on a certain day to carry out their purpose, sharpening their horns for the conquest, until a very old ox who had long ploughed the fields spoke. "These butchers, it is true, slaughter us," he said, "but they do so with skillful hands and no unnecessary pain. If we get rid of them, we might fall into the hands of botchers and suffer a double death, for you may be assured that men will never go without beef."

Better the devil you know than one you don't.

THE DOG IN THE MANGER

A Dog lay in a manger, growling and snarling so much that he prevented the oxen from eating the hay that had been placed there for them. "What a selfish Dog!" said one ox to his companions. "He doesn't eat hay himself, but he refuses to allow those to eat who can."

THE GNAT AND THE BULL

A Gnat settled on the horn of a Bull and sat there a time before asking if his presence was inconveniencing the great beast. The Bull replied, "I didn't even know you were there, so it doesn't matter to me if you go or stay."

Some men are of more consequence in their own eyes than in the eyes of their neighbors.

THE MICE IN COUNCIL

The Mice called a council to decide how they might best fight back against the persecution of their great enemy, the Cat. The plan that found most favor was the proposal to tie a bell to the neck of the Cat, so that the Mice would be warned by the sound of his approach. But when the Mice further debated who among them should hang the bell, no one would agree to do it.

It is one thing to propose and another to execute.

THE LION AND THE GOAT

On a summer's day when all the beasts were suffering from extreme heat, a Lion and a Goat came at the same time to quench their thirst at a small fountain. They at once fell to quarrelling over who should drink first, until it became apparent that neither would give in. But, ceasing argument for a moment to recover their breath, they saw a flock of Vultures hovering overhead, waiting to pounce upon whichever of the two should be the first to die of thirst. Whereupon they instantly made up their quarrel, agreeing that it was far better to be friends than to become food for the Vultures.

THE TWO POTS

Two Pots, one made of earthenware and the other of brass, were carried down a river during a flood. The Brazen Pot told his companion to keep by his side for protection. "Thanks for your offer," said the Earthen Pot, "but actually what I'm afraid of is you. If you touch me even slightly, I'm sure I'll break into pieces. But if you keep at a distance, I may float down in safety."

Equals make the best friends. Avoid neighbors who are too powerful.

§

THE DOCTOR AND HIS PATIENT

A Doctor had been for some time attending a sick man who, nevertheless, died under his hands. At the funeral the Doctor went about among the relations, saying, "Our poor friend—if he had only refrained from wine, attended to his digestion and taken proper care, he would not be lying there." One of the mourners answered him, "My good sir, it is of no use to say this now; you ought to have made these prescriptions when your Patient was alive to hear them."

The best advice may come too late.

THE BEE AND JUPITER

A Queen Bee from Mount Hymettus flew to Olympus to present to Jupiter some honey fresh from her combs. Jupiter, so delighted with the gift, promised to give the Queen whatever she wanted. She thought and said, "Give me, please, a stinger with which I can kill any mortal who tries to take my honey." Jupiter was much displeased, for he loved mankind, but he could not refuse the request. So he answered the Bee, "You shall have your request, but it will be at the peril of your own life. If you use your stinger, it will remain in the wound you make, and you will die from the loss of it."

He that wishes evil for his neighbor brings a curse upon himself.

☾

THE HUNTSMAN AND THE FISHERMAN

A Huntsman, returning from the field, fell in by chance with a Fisherman who was bringing home a basket laden with his catch. The Huntsman had a craving for fish, and the Fisherman preferred a supper of game, so they quickly agreed to exchange the product of their day's work. Each was so pleased with his change in diet that they made the same exchange day after day. A neighbor said to them, "If you go on in this way, you will soon destroy the pleasure of your exchange, and each will want to keep the fruits of his own sport."

Absence makes the heart grow fonder.

THE GOOSE WHO
LAID THE GOLDEN EGGS

A cottager and his wife possessed a Goose that laid every day a Golden Egg. But, dissatisfied with so slow an income and thinking the Goose was full of gold, they decided to kill it and seize the whole treasure at once. Cutting her open, they discovered the Goose differed in no respect from their others.

Much wants more and loses all.

THE MOUNTEBANK
AND THE COUNTRYMAN

A wealthy patrician, intending to treat the Roman people to theatrical entertainment, publicly offered a reward to anyone who could produce a novel spectacle. Artists arrived from all parts to claim the prize, among them a well-known and witty Mountebank who said he had a new kind of entertainment that had never yet been produced on any stage. This report brought the whole city out, and the theater could hardly contain the number of spectators. When the artist appeared alone on the stage, without any apparatus or assistants, suspense kept the spectators in profound silence. Suddenly he thrust down his head into his bosom, as if he might have something hidden there, and mimicked the squeaking of a young pig so naturally that the audience insisted he must be hiding one under his cloak. They called for him to be searched, and when no pig was found, they lauded him with the most extravagant applause.

A Countryman in the audience said he could do better and announced that he would perform the next day. Accordingly, an even greater crowd gathered; prejudiced in favor of the Mountebank, they came more to laugh at the Countryman than to see what he could offer. Both men came out upon the stage, and the Mountebank grunted away first, again receiving thunderous applause. Then the Countryman, acting as if he also concealed something under his garments, gave out a pig-like squeak. The people cried out that the Mountebank had imitated a pig much better and hooted to the Countryman to quit the stage; but, to their surprise, he produced a real pig from his bosom. "And now, gentlemen, you see," he said, "what kind of judges you are!"

It is easier to convince a man against his senses than against his will.

THE DOG INVITED
TO SUPPER

A rich man gave a great feast to which he invited many friends and acquaintances. His Dog availed himself of the occasion to invite a friend, too, saying, "My master is planning a feast; come and sup with me tonight. You will have unusually good cheer." The Invited Dog went at the hour appointed and, seeing the preparations in the kitchen for so grand an entertainment, said to himself with joy, "How glad I am that I came! I do not often get such a chance as this. I will eat enough to last me both today and tomorrow." While thinking this he wagged his tail and gave a sly look to the friend who had invited him. All the wagging caught the Cook's eye, and, seizing him by his paws, the Cook threw the overanxious dog out the window. He fell heavily to the ground and limped off, howling dreadfully. His yelling soon attracted the other street dogs, who inquired how he had enjoyed his supper. He replied, "Why, to tell you the truth, I drank so much wine that I remember nothing. I don't even know how I got out of the house."

Those who enter by the backstairs may expect to be shown out by the window.

THE GOATHERD AND THE
WILD GOATS

A Goatherd, driving his flock from their pasture one evening, found some Wild Goats mingled among them and shut them up together with his own for the night. The next day it snowed very hard, so that he could not take the herd to their feeding places. He gave his own goats just sufficient food to keep them alive, but he fed the strangers more, hoping to entice them to stay and become part of his flock. When the thaw came, he led them all out again to feed, and the Wild Goats scampered away as fast as they could. Furious at their ingratitude, the Goatherd yelled after them. One of the Wild Goats turned about and said, "If yesterday you treated us better than the goats you have had so long, than no doubt you would someday treat us shabbily, too."

THE FROGS
ASKING FOR A KING

The Frogs petitioned Jupiter to appoint them a King to keep them organized and make them lead more honest lives. Jupiter, who felt they needed no King, tried to appease them by casting down a huge log into the lake and declaring it their King. The frogs, terrified by the

splash the log made, hid themselves in the depths of the pool. After a while, however, they noticed that their new ruler remained motionless, and they soon became brave enough to climb up and squat upon it. After some time they began to think themselves ill served by the appointment of so tame a King, and they sent a second delegation to Jupiter, asking him to send another sovereign. He then appointed an eel to govern them. When the frogs discovered their second King's easy good nature, they went a third time to Jupiter to beg that he choose a more suitable leader. Jupiter, displeased by their complaints, sent a heron, who devoured the frogs one by one. The few who escaped asked Mercury to take a note to Jupiter asking for help; but Jupiter replied that they were being punished for their folly and that they should learn to leave well enough alone.

THE ASS AND HIS MASTERS

An Ass, finding himself in the service of a gardener who gave him too little food and too much work, asked Jupiter to provide him with another master. Jupiter, warning the Ass that he might regret his request, sent him to a potter. Shortly afterwards, finding that he had heavier loads to carry and harder work in the brick field, the Ass petitioned for another change of master. Jupiter, telling the beast that this would be the last time he could make such a request, arranged for him to be sold to a tanner. The Ass, finding that he had fallen into even worse hands, said sadly, "I should have stayed where I was. Even after I am dead my present owner will make me useful to him—by tanning my hide."

He who is discontented in one place will seldom be happy in another.

THE THIEF AND THE DOG

A Thief coming to burglarize a house thought he might stop the barking of its Dog by throwing the beast several slices of meat. "Away with you," said the Dog. "I was suspicious of you before, but this extravagance convinces me that you are a rogue."

A bribe in hand betrays mischief at heart.

THE BEES, THE DRONES, AND THE WASP

Some Bees had built their comb in the hollow trunk of an oak. The Drones asserted that they had made the nest and that it belonged to them. The cause was brought into court before the Wasp. Knowing something of the parties, he said, "The plaintiffs and defendants are so much alike in shape and color as to render ownership a doubtful matter. Therefore, let each party take a hive to itself and build a new comb, so that I can tell from the shape of the cells and the taste of the honey who are the rightful owners of the property in dispute." The Bees readily assented to the Wasp's plan, while the Drones declined it. "It is clear now who made the comb," said the Wasp, "and who cannot make one."

THE LION AND THE ASS HUNTING

A Lion and an Ass made an agreement to go out hunting together. By and by they came to a cave where many wild goats lived. The Lion took up his station at the mouth of the cave, and the Ass, going inside, kicked and brayed and made a mighty fuss to frighten the goats out. After the Lion had caught a great number of them, the Ass came out and asked if he had not made a noble fight and routed the goats properly. "Yes, indeed," said the Lion. "I assure you, you would have frightened me, too, if I had not known you to be an Ass."

When braggarts are invited into the company of their betters, it is only to be made use of and laughed at.

THE LARK AND
HER YOUNG ONES

A Lark had made her nest in a field of corn. The brood had almost grown to full size when, one day, as their mother was away searching for food, the Owner of the field came to look over his crop. Finding it ripe, he said, "The time has come when I must ask my neighbors to help me with my harvest." One of the young birds heard this speech and related it to his mother, asking her where they should move their nest. "There is no reason to move yet, my son," she replied. "The man who only has friends help him with his harvest is not really serious." The Owner of the field came again a few days later and, finding the sun hotter and the corn riper, said, "I will come myself tomorrow with my laborers, and with as many reapers as I can hire, and bring in the harvest." The Lark, on hearing these words, said to her brood, "Now it is time to go, my little ones, for the man is in earnest this time; he no longer trusts his friends, but will reap the field himself."

Self-help is the best help.

THE LION
AND THE DOLPHIN

A Lion roaming by the sea saw a Dolphin lift its head out of the waves and decided to ask him to form an alliance. The Lion told the Dolphin that, since one was the king of beasts on the earth, and the other was the ruler of all the creatures of the ocean, they ought to be best friends. The Dolphin gladly consented. Not long afterwards the Lion had a difficult battle with a wild bull and called on his new ally to help. But the Dolphin, though quite willing, was unable to assist, as he could not reach the land. The Lion accused him of betrayal, and the Dolphin replied, "Don't blame me, but rather my nature, which, however powerful at sea, is completely helpless on land."

In choosing allies look to their power as well as their will to aid.

THE BIRDS,
THE BEASTS, AND THE BAT

Once there was a fierce war between the Birds and the Beasts, and each party was by turns the conqueror. A Bat, uncertain of the outcome of the fight, always aligned himself with the side that was the strongest at the time. When peace was proclaimed, the Bat's deceitful conduct was apparent to both parties. He was forced to go off by himself and has since lived in holes and corners, never daring to show his face except in the duskiness of twilight.

THE FOX AND THE HEDGEHOG

A Fox, while crossing a river, was driven into a narrow gorge by the rushing water and lay there a long time, unable to get out and covered with countless horseflies. A wandering Hedgehog spied the Fox and, taking pity on him, asked if he should drive away the flies. "Please, no," cried the Fox. "The flies who are on me are already full; if you remove them, a swarm of hungry ones will come and leave not a drop of blood in my body."

When we throw off rulers who have already made the most of us, we lay ourselves open to others who will surely make us bleed more freely.

THE WOLF AND THE SHEPHERD

A Wolf followed a flock of sheep for a long time but did not hurt any of them. The Shepherd at first stood on his guard and kept a strict watch over the Wolf's movements. But when the Wolf, day after day, made not the slightest effort to seize the sheep, the Shepherd began to look upon him as a friend rather than a foe, and when occasion called him one day into the city, he left the sheep in the Wolf's charge. Now that he had the opportunity, the Wolf fell upon the sheep and destroyed most of the flock. On his return the Shepherd exclaimed, "I got what I deserved, trusting my sheep to a Wolf!"

There is more danger in an insincere friend than an open enemy.

THE TWO TRAVELLERS AND THE AXE

Two men were travelling together when one of them, spying a hatchet, cried, "See what I found!" "Do not say *I*," said the other. "Say look what *we* found." After a while the Travellers came across the men who had lost the hatchet; immediately they accused the first man, who held it, of theft. "Alas," he said to his friend, "we are undone!" "Do not say *we*," replied the other. "Say *I* am undone. You can't expect me to share in the danger if I was not to share in the prize."

THE WEASELS AND THE MICE

The Weasels and the Mice had long been at war, and much blood had been shed. As the Weasels were always the victors, the Mice thought that the cause of their frequent defeats was lack of discipline and the fact that they had no leaders in the army. They chose as commanders those most renowned for their family descent, strength, counsel, and courage. With the leaders in place and the army disciplined, the Weasels and Mice again proclaimed war, and the newly chosen generals bound their heads with straws so that they might be more noticeable to their troops. Scarcely had the battle commenced when the opposition overwhelmed the Mice, who scampered off as fast as they could to their holes. The generals, not being able to move quickly into safety because of the ornaments on their heads, were captured and devoured by the Weasels.

There is no distinction without its accompanying danger.

THE BOY AND THE NETTLE

A Boy who was stung by a Nettle ran home and told his mother, saying, "I barely touched it and it stung me anyway." "That is exactly the trouble," said his mother. "The next time you touch a Nettle, grasp it boldly, and it will be soft as silk to your hand."

Do boldly what you do at all.

THE TRUMPETER
TAKEN PRISONER

A Trumpeter, bravely leading on his fellow soldiers, was captured by the enemy. He cried out to his captors, "Please spare me. I have not killed a single man myself. I am unarmed and carry nothing but this trumpet." "That is the very reason why you should be put to death," they said. "For, while you do not fight yourself, your trumpet stirs others to battle."

He who incites strife is as bad as those who take part in it.

THE SICK KITE

A Kite who had long been ill said to his mother, "Don't cry, mother, but go and pray to the gods for my recovery." She replied, "Alas! Which god do you think I should ask? Are there any whom you have not outraged by stealing sacrifices from their altars?"

Make friends in prosperity to have their help in adversity.

THE EAGLE AND THE JACKDAW

An Eagle, flying down from his nest on a high rock, carried off a lamb. A Jackdaw who witnessed the capture was green with envy and decided to emulate the Eagle. He flew round with a great flapping of his wings and settled upon a large Ram, which he tried to carry off. But the Jackdaw's claws became entangled in the Ram's fleece and, though he fluttered his feathers as much as he could, he was not able to free himself. The Shepherd, seeing what had happened, ran up and caught him. He clipped the Jackdaw's wings and gave the bird to his children that night. When they asked, "Father, what kind of bird is it?" the Shepherd replied, "He thinks he is an Eagle, but take my word for it—he's a Jackdaw."

THE ASS AND HIS DRIVER

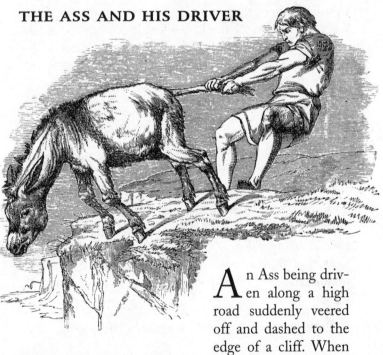

An Ass being driven along a high road suddenly veered off and dashed to the edge of a cliff. When he was right at the point of falling over, his owner seized him by the tail and tried to pull him back. But the Ass resisted his efforts. The man gave up and said, "If you insist on being the master, there's nothing I can do. A willful beast must go his own way."

THE PARTRIDGE
AND THE FALCONER

A Falconer caught a Partridge in his net and was about to kill it when the Partridge cried out sorrowfully, "Please let me go, Mr. Falconer, and I promise I will decoy other partridges into your net." The Falconer replied, "I shall now feel less sorry about taking your life, because you are willing to save it at the cost of betraying your friends."

THE FIR TREE AND THE BRAMBLE

A Fir Tree was one day boasting to a Bramble, "You are good for nothing at all, while I will be used to build barns and houses." The Bramble answered, "You poor creature—if you could only picture the axes and saws that are about to hew you down, you would have reason to wish that you had grown up a Bramble instead."

Better poverty without care than riches with.

THE OLD MAN AND DEATH

An Old Man who had traveled a long way with a huge pile of wood found himself so weary that he had to stop. He put the bundle down and called upon Death to take him away from his miserable existence. Death came immediately and asked the Old Man what he wanted. "Pray, good sir," said he, "could you do me the favor of helping me pick up my burden?"

It is one thing to call for Death and another to see him coming.

THE STAG AND THE VINE

A Stag being pursued by hunters hid himself beneath the large leaves of a Vine. The huntsmen passed by without discovering him, and when the Stag thought all was safe, he began to nibble at the Vine's tendrils. But one of the huntsmen, attracted by the rustling of the leaves, looked back and, guessing that their prey was hiding, shot an arrow from his bow. As he was dying the Stag groaned, "I deserve this, for I should not have mistreated the Vine that saved me."

THE MISER

A Miser sold all his property and goods to buy a lump of gold, which he buried in a hole in the ground by the side of an old wall. Daily he went to visit it, and one of his workmen observed his frequent appearances at the spot. When the master was gone the workman dug down, found the lump of gold, and stole it. On his next visit the Miser found the hole empty and began to wail and tear out his hair. A neighbor, learning the cause of his grief, said, "Take a stone and place it in the hole, then pretend that the gold is still lying there. As you never meant to use it, one will do you as much good as the other."

The worth of money is not in its possession, but in its use.

THE OLD WOMAN
AND HER MAIDS

A thrifty Old Woman kept two servant girls and expected them to begin work in the morning as soon as the cock crowed. The Maids disliked this early rising and decided to wring the cock's neck to prevent him from waking their mistress so early. But the Old Woman, missing her usual alarm, continually mistook the hour and roused the Maids in the middle of the night.

Cunning too often overreaches itself.

THE LION, THE BEAR,
AND THE FOX

A Lion and a Bear both found the carcass of a Fawn and fought fiercely for its possession. When they had badly injured each other and were faint from the long combat, they lay down, too tired to touch the prize. A Fox who was passing by saw them stretched out on the ground, with the Fawn lying untouched in the middle, and seized the kid for himself. The Lion and the Bear, too helpless to get up, said, "How pathetic that we have fought merely to give a rogue a dinner!"

It sometimes happens that one man does all the work and another takes all the profit.

THE FARMER AND THE CRANES

Some Cranes settled down in a Farmer's field that was newly sown. For a while the Farmer frightened them away by brandishing an empty sling. But when the Cranes found out that he was only bluffing, they no longer bothered to fly off. The Farmer then began to sling at the Cranes with stones and killed a great many of them. The rest flew off to Lilliput, saying "This man is no longer content just to scare us, but is determined to get rid of us for real."

If words don't suffice, blows must follow.

THE SICK LION

A Lion, being weak from old age, found it harder to obtain food by force and resolved to do so by artifice. He kept to his den and pretended to be sick, taking care that his sickness should be publicly known. The beasts expressed their sorrow and came one by one to his den to visit, and the Lion devoured each one. After many of the animals had disappeared, the Fox presented himself to the Lion, standing on the outside of the cave at a respectful distance. He asked the Lion how he was feeling, and the king of beasts replied, "I am no better, but why do you stand out there? Please come inside to talk." The Fox said, "No, thank you. I notice that there are many footprints entering your cave, but no signs of any leaving."

He is wise who is warned by the misfortunes of others.

THE BOASTING TRAVELLER

A man who had travelled in foreign lands boasted, on returning to his own country, of the wonderful and heroic things he had done on his journeys. He said, for instance, that in Rhodes he had taken an extraordinary leap that no man could better, and that he had witnesses there to prove it. Interrupting him, one of the bystanders said, "My good man, you don't need any witnesses. Pretend this is Rhodes and try the leap again."

THE WOLF IN SHEEP'S CLOTHING

Once upon a time a Wolf decided to disguise himself, thinking this would make it easier to get food. Clothing himself in the skin of a sheep, he joined a flock and fed along with them, fooling even the shepherd. In the evening he was shut up with the sheep in the fold, and the gate was locked. When the shepherd got hungry later that night, he went back to the fold to choose his dinner. Instead of a sheep, though, he picked the Wolf and ate him on the spot.

THE WOLF AND THE HORSE

A Wolf coming out of a field of oats met a Horse and told him, "Take your supper in that field. It is full of excellent oats, which I have left for you untouched." The Horse replied, "If you wolves could eat oats, I doubt you'd be so happy to share your discovery."

Few thanks are due to those who give away what is of no use to them.

THE BOY AND THE FILBERTS

A Boy put his hand into a pitcher full of Filberts. He grasped as many as he could possibly hold, but when he tried to pull his hand out, the narrowness of the pitcher's neck prevented him. Unwilling to lose his Filberts, and yet unable to withdraw his hand, he burst into tears and bitterly lamented his predicament. A bystander said to him, "Grasp only half of what you have, my boy, and you will easily succeed."

Do not attempt too much at once.

THE FOX AND THE MASK

A Fox broke into the house of an actor and, rummaging through his belongings, came upon a mask, a clever likeness of a human head. The Fox placed his paws on it and said, "What a beautiful head! What a pity that it's missing a brain."

A pretty shell is a poor substitute for inward substance.

THE RAVEN AND THE SWAN

A Raven envied the whiteness of a Swan's plumage and, thinking that the Swan's beauty derived from the water in which she lived, he deserted his home for the pools and streams. There he plumed himself and washed his coat, but his feathers remained as black as ever; and, not finding his usual food in this new location, the Raven soon died of starvation.

Change of scene is not change of nature.

THE HEIFER AND THE OX

A Heifer who ran wild in the fields and had never felt the yoke, criticized an Ox pulling a plough for submitting to such drudgery. The Ox said nothing and continued his work. Soon after there was a great festival, and while the Ox was allowed to celebrate, the Heifer was led off to be sacrificed at the altar. The Ox saw what was being done and, with a smile, told the Heifer, "You were allowed to live in idleness because you were going to be sacrificed."

THE LION AND
THE THREE BULLS

For a long time three Bulls pastured together in peace and amity. A Lion lay in ambush hoping to make them his prey, but he was afraid to attack the Bulls while they kept together. Instead, the Lion began to spread evil and scandalous reports pitting one Bull against another, and he soon succeeded in separating them. He then attacked them without fear as they ate alone and feasted on the Bulls at his leisure.

The quarrels of friends are the opportunities of foes.

THE THIRSTY PIGEON

A Pigeon, uncomfortable from excessive thirst, saw a glass of water painted on a sign. Not realizing it was only a picture, she flew towards the water at top speed and crashed against the board. She broke her wings with the blow and fell to the ground, where she was caught by a passer-by.

Great haste is not always good speed.

THE GOAT AND THE GOATHERD

A Goatherd tried to bring a stray Goat back to his flock. He whistled and called out, but the straggler paid no attention. At last the Goatherd threw a stone and broke the Goat's horn. Alarmed at what he had done, he begged the creature not to tell his master. The Goat replied, "Oh, you silly fellow—the horn will speak even if I am silent."

Facts speak plainer than words.

THE HOUND AND THE HARE

A Hound was chasing a Hare for some time, and when the dog at last caught up to her, he began biting and then licking her. The Hare, not knowing what to make of this behavior, said, "If you are a friend, why bite me? And if you're a foe, why caress me?"

Let a man be one thing or another, and then we know where we stand.

THE CAMEL AND THE ARAB

An Arab loaded up his Camel and then asked the beast which he would prefer, to go uphill or downhill. "Pray, master," said the Camel dryly, "what is wrong with the straight way across the plain?"

THE ASS CARRYING THE IMAGE

An Ass who was carrying an Image in a religious procession noticed that he was bowed to by all the people he passed. The Ass, thinking the worship was for himself, bristled with pride and soon refused to take another step. But the driver hit the Ass across the back with his stick, saying, "You silly dolt! It is not you they honor but the Image that you carry!"

Fools claim for themselves the respect that is given to their office.

☾

THE FOX AND THE STORK

A Fox invited a Stork to supper but served only
some thin soup in a flat stone dish. The soup fell
out of the long bill of the Stork at every mouthful, and
his vexation at not being able to eat provided the Fox
with intense amusement. In turn the Stork asked the
Fox to dine with him and set before her a flagon with
a long, narrow mouth. The Stork could easily insert his
neck and enjoy the contents, while the Fox was obli-
ged to content himself with licking the neck of the jar.
Unable to satisfy his hunger, the Fox left with good
grace, knowing he could hardly find fault with his host
for paying him back with his own coin.

THE ASS IN THE LION'S SKIN

An Ass put on a Lion's Skin and roamed the forest, amusing himself by frightening all the innocent animals he met. Seeing a Fox, the Ass tried to frighten him also. But the Fox, who had heard the Ass's voice, exclaimed, "I might have been frightened, too, if I had not heard you bray."

THE BALD KNIGHT

A Bald Knight who wore a wig went out to hunt. When a sudden puff of wind exposed his bald pate, a loud laugh rang forth from the Knight's companions. He pulled up his horse and joined in the joke by saying, "How could I expect to keep strange hair on my head when my own would not stay there!"

THE ASS AND HIS SHADOW

A Traveller hired an Ass to carry him from Athens to Megara. At midday the heat of the sun was so intense that the Traveller stopped to rest and wanted to shelter himself from the heat in the shadow of the Ass. But the Driver of the Ass had the same idea, and the beast could only provide shade for one. A violent dispute arose between them; the Driver maintained that he had hired out the Ass only, and not his shadow, while the Traveller asserted that he had hired both. While they were wrangling, the Ass took to his heels and was soon out of reach.

When worrying about the shadow we often lose the substance.

THE BULL AND THE GOAT

A Bull being pursued by a Lion fled into a cave where a Wild Goat had also taken refuge. The Goat began to attack the Bull, butting him with his horns. "I'll take your abuse now," said the Bull, "but don't think that it is you I am afraid of. As soon as the Lion is out of sight, I will show you the difference between a Bull and a Goat."

It shows an evil disposition to take advantage of those in distress.

ℰ

THE QUACK FROG

A Frog once emerged from his swamp home and announced to all the beasts that he was a learned physician, skilled in the use of drugs and able to cure all diseases. A Fox asked him, "How can you help others when you are unable to fix your own limping gait or restore your own wrinkled skin?"

Physician, heal thyself.

THE HORSE
AND THE LOADED ASS

A Man who kept a Horse and an Ass tried to spare
the Horse in his journeys, putting all the burden
upon the Ass's back. The Ass, who had been ailing for
some time, asked the Horse one day to help him with
part of the load. "If you will only take a fair portion,"
said the Ass, "I will soon get well; but if you refuse to
help, this weight will kill me." The Horse, however, told
the Ass not to trouble him with complaints. The Ass
jogged on in silence, but presently, overcome with the
weight of his burden, he dropped down dead. The master then took the load from the dead Ass, as well as the
Ass's carcass, and put them on the Horse's back. "Alas,"

said the Horse, "since I refused to bear my portion of the load, I must now carry it all, and a dead weight, too."

A disobliging temper creates its own punishment.

THE VINE AND THE GOAT

A spoiled Goat, coming upon a Vine teeming with ripe fruit and tender shoots, stopped to gnaw the bark and browse among the young leaves. "I will get my revenge for this insult," said the Vine to the Goat. "For it will be the juice of my grapes that will be poured over your forehead when you are sacrificed upon the altar."

Retribution, though late, comes at last.

THE SWALLOW
AND THE COURT OF JUSTICE

A Swallow built her nest under the eaves of a Court of Justice. One day, before her young ones could fly, a Serpent discovered the nest and ate them all. When the poor bird returned to her nest and found it empty, she began to wail. A neighbor, trying to comfort the Swallow, mentioned that she was not the first bird to have lost her young. "True," she replied, "but it is not just my little ones I mourn, but also the fact that I have been wronged in the very place where the injured go for justice."

THE WOLF AND THE GOAT

A Wolf saw a Goat feeding at the summit of a steep cliff, where he had no chance of reaching her. The Wolf called to her and earnestly suggested that the Goat come down lower so as not to fall and hurt herself. He added that the meadows where he was standing were quite sweet and abundant. She replied, "No, my friend—it is not for *my* dinner that you invite me, but for your own."

THE MAN AND HIS TWO WIVES

I n days when men were allowed more than one wife, a middle-aged Man whose hair was just turning gray fell in love with two women at once and married them both. One was young and blooming and wanted her husband to appear as youthful as she; the other was somewhat older and preferred that her husband look her age. So while the young one pulled out the Man's gray hairs, the older one was equally industrious in plucking out his black strands. The Man enjoyed their attention and devotion until he found that, between them, he had not a hair left on his head.

Those who seek to please everybody, please no one.

THE SALT MERCHANT
AND HIS ASS

A Merchant who dealt in salt drove his Ass to the seashore, where salt could be bought more cheaply. On the way home, the Ass took a misstep and fell into a stream; when he rose up again his load was considerably lighter, as the water had melted the salt. The peddler went back to the seashore and filled his baskets with a larger quantity of salt than before. When he came again to the stream, the Ass fell down on purpose, hoping to lighten his load again. Regaining his feet with the weight of the load much diminished, he brayed triumphantly. The man saw through the trick, however, and drove him for a third time to the coast, where the Merchant bought a cargo of sponges instead of salt. When the Ass reached the stream, he fell down once more; but when the sponges became swollen with water, his load doubled in weight.

The same measures will not suit all circumstances, and we may play the same trick once too often.

THE STAG
AT THE POOL

O ne summer's day a Stag
came to a pool to quench
his thirst and, as he stood
drinking, saw his form reflected in the water. "What beauty
and strength are in these horns
of mine," he said, "but how

unseemly are my weak and slender feet." While he was criticizing the form with which nature had provided him, a huntsman and his hounds grew near. The feet he had belittled carried him away from his pursuers, but the horns he was so proud of became entangled in a thicket and held him there for the hunter.

Look to use before beauty.

THE ASTRONOMER

An Astronomer used to go out each night to observe the stars. One evening, as he wandered through the outskirts of town with his attention on the sky, he fell into a deep well. When he cried loudly for help, a neighbor ran to the well and, learning what had happened, said, "You poor man—while prying into the mysteries of heaven, you overlook the common objects underneath your feet."

THE SHEPHERD
AND THE SEA

A Shepherd who tended a flock by the calm sea developed a strong desire to sail. He sold his sheep, bought a cargo of dates, and set sail. He had not gone far when a storm arose and the ship was wrecked, spilling the dates into the sea; the man escaped with only his life. Not long after, when the sea was again calm, one of the Shepherd's friends admired its beauty, to which the Shepherd replied, "Beware of that smooth surface. The sea is again looking for some dates."

THE KID AND THE WOLF

A Kid, returning without protection from the pasture, was pursued by a Wolf. He turned around and said to the Wolf, "I know, friend Wolf, that I am your victim, but before I die, I ask you one favor—to play me a tune to which I may dance." The Wolf complied, and while he was piping, the hounds, hearing the music, came up and chased the Wolf away.

He who steps out of character to play the fool should not expect to win the prize.

THE RIVERS AND THE SEA

The Rivers joined together to complain to the Sea, saying, "Why is it that when we flow into your tides so drinkable and sweet, you work a change on us, making us salty and unfit to drink?" The Sea, in an attempt to appease them, said, "If you don't wish to become salty, then keep away from me altogether."

Some find fault with those things by which they are chiefly benefited.

THE FISHERMAN AND HIS NET

A Fisherman was drawing up his Net and found he had captured a great haul of fish. He managed to retain all the large fish in the Net and drew them to the shore, but he found that the smaller fish had fallen through the mesh back into the sea.

Our insignificance is often the cause of our safety.

THE BLACKSMITH
AND HIS DOG

A Blacksmith had a little Dog who was his constant companion. While the Blacksmith hammered away at his metals, the Dog slept; but whenever the man sat down to dinner, the Dog woke up and wagged his tail. "Sluggard cur!" said the master one day, throwing the Dog a bone. "You sleep through the noise of the anvil but wake up at the first clatter of my teeth."

Men are awake to their own interests.

THE LION IN A FARMYARD

One day a Lion entered a Farmyard. The Farmer, wishing to catch him, shut the gate. When the Lion found he could not escape, he jumped upon the sheep and killed them, then attacked the oxen. So the Farmer, beginning to worry for his own safety, opened the gate, and the Lion made off as fast as he could. Afterward the Farmer lamented the destruction of his sheep and oxen, while his wife, who had seen all that took place, said, "How could you even think of shutting up a Lion with you in the Farmyard, when you shake in your shoes if you even hear his roar at a distance?"

It is better to scare a thief than to snare him.

THE WILD BOAR AND THE FOX

A Wild Boar stood under a tree, rubbing his tusks against the trunk. A Fox passing by asked him why he was sharpening his teeth when there seemed to be no danger from huntsman or hound. He replied, "I do it as good measure. It would never do to be sharpening my weapons just at the time I ought to be using them."

It is too late to polish the sword when the trumpet sounds to draw it.

THE ASS, THE COCK,
AND THE LION

An Ass and a Cock lived on a farm together. One day a Lion, desperate from hunger, approached the barnyard. He was about to spring upon the Ass when the Cock crowed loudly, and the Lion, who is said to hate the sound of a Cock's crow, dashed away as fast as he could. The Ass, observing the Lion's trepidation at the mere crowing of a Cock, summoned up the courage to attack him and galloped off in pursuit. He had run only a short distance, however, when the Lion turned around and seized him.

Presumption, begun in ignorance, ends in ruin.

THE CHARGER AND THE ASS

A Charger, adorned with fine trappings, came thundering along the road, inspiring envy in a poor Ass who was trudging along with a heavy load upon his back. "Get out of my way!" said the proud Horse, "or I'll trample you under my feet." The Ass said nothing and moved to the side of the road. Not long afterward the Charger was wounded in battle and sent to work on a farm. When the Ass saw the Horse drawing a dung cart, he began to ridicule him. Then he realized that, for someone so overbearing in times of prosperity, it was just punishment for the Charger to have lost any friends who could aid in time of need.

THE MOUSE
AND THE WEASEL

A starving little Mouse made his way with some difficulty through a hole in a basket of corn. Once inside, he found the food so delicious that he stuffed himself; but when he tried to get out, he discovered that the hole was too small for his puffed-up body. A Weasel, hearing his frustrated cries, said, "You'll have to wait and fast till you are thin, for you will never get out till you get back to the same size as you were when you entered."

THE EAGLE AND THE BEETLE

The Eagle and the Beetle were at war. The Eagle started the battle by seizing and eating the Beetle's young ones. The Beetle then secretly got to the Eagle's eggs and rolled them out of the nest. The Eagle made a complaint to Jupiter, who offered the Eagle his lap to use as a safe nest. While Jupiter had the eggs in his lap, however, the Beetle came buzzing around his head. Jupiter rose up to drive the Beetle away and dropped the nest, breaking all of the eggs.

The weak often revenge themselves on those who mistreat them, even when the other is more powerful.

THE FOX
AND THE LEOPARD

The Fox and the Leopard disagreed over who was the more beautiful. The Leopard exhibited the numerous spots that decorated his skin, but the Fox replied, "It is better to have a versatile mind than a variegated body."

THE WOLF AND THE LION

A Wolf stole a lamb from a fold and was carrying her off to his lair. A Lion met him in the path and seized the lamb from him. The Wolf, taken aback, cried out that the Lion was a thief. The Lion jeeringly replied, "I suppose, then, that the shepherd *gave* you the lamb?"

THE OLD LION

A Lion, worn out from illness and old age, lay on the ground at the point of death. A Boar came up and, avenging an old grudge, attacked him with his tusks. Later a Bull, also eager for retaliation, gored him with his horns. When the Ass saw that the huge beast could be attacked without punishment, he kicked him in the forehead. The dying Lion said, "The insults of the powerful were bad enough, but to be assaulted by a creature as base as you is to die twice."

THE WOLF
AND THE SHEPHERDS

A Wolf passing by saw some Shepherds in a hut eating a joint of mutton for dinner. Approaching them, he said, "What a clamor you would raise if I were to do as you are doing!"

Men are quick to condemn in others the very things that they themselves practice.

THE SEASIDE TRAVELLERS

Some Travellers, journeying along the shore, climbed to the summit of a tall cliff to look out over the sea. They saw in the distance what they thought was a large ship and waited in the hope of seeing it enter the harbor. But as the distant object was driven nearer to the shore, they decided that it could at most be a small boat. And when it finally reached the beach, they discovered that it was only a large bundle of sticks. One of the Travellers said to his companions, "We have waited for no reason—there is nothing to see but a faggot."

Our anticipations of life often outrun its realities.

THE DOGS AND THE HIDES

Some Dogs, famished with hunger, saw some cow Hides a skinner had left on the bottom of a stream. Not being able to reach them, the Dogs decided to try drinking up the river; but long before they reached the Hides, they all burst themselves with water.

Attempt not impossibilities.

THE ANT AND THE DOVE

An Ant went to the bank of a river to quench his thirst and tumbled in. He was carried away by the rush of the stream and was about to drown when a Dove, sitting on a tree overhanging the water, plucked a leaf and let it fall into the stream close to him. The Ant, climbing onto it, floated in safety to the bank. Shortly afterwards a birdcatcher was standing under the tree, laying a net to trap the Dove. The Ant, perceiving the man's intentions, bit him on the foot. The surprise made the man drop his net, and the Dove, warned of the danger, flew off.

One good turn deserves another.

THE FOX
AND THE CROW

A Crow, having stolen a bit of flesh, perched in a tree and held it in her beak. A Fox spied the morsel and longed to possess it. "How handsome is the Crow," he deceitfully exclaimed, "in the beauty of her shape and the fairness of her complexion! Oh, if her voice were only equal to her beauty, she would be considered the Queen of Birds!" The Crow, anxious to defend the attack made upon her voice, gave out a loud caw and dropped the flesh. The Fox quickly picked it up and walked off, saying that, although he had complimented the Crow's beauty, he had nothing to say about her brains.

Men seldom flatter without some ulterior motive, and those who listen to such music may expect to pay the piper.

THE THREE TRADESMEN

A great city was expecting to be besieged, and its inhabitants were called together to discuss the best means of protecting themselves from the enemy. A Bricklayer recommended bricks as the best materials, while a Carpenter proposed timber as far preferable. Then a Currier stood and said, "Sirs, I disagree with you both; there is nothing in the world so good as leather."

Every man for himself.

THE BOY BATHING

A Boy who was bathing in a river drifted into deep water and was about to drown. He called out to a Traveller passing by, asking him for help. The man began to scold the Boy for his foolhardiness, but the youth cried out, "Rescue me now, sir, and save the lecture for later."

Counsel without aid is useless.

VENUS AND THE CAT

A Cat fell in love with a handsome young man and begged Venus to change her into a woman. Venus agreed to her request and transformed her into a beautiful damsel. When the youth saw her, he fell in love and took her home as his bride. While the couple were relaxing in their house, Venus, wanting to discover if the Cat had been altogether transformed, placed a mouse in the middle of the room. The woman, forgetting her present condition, jumped up from the couch and pursued the mouse as if she would eat it on the spot. Venus, much disappointed, turned the Cat back to her former shape.

Nature exceeds nurture.

THE FARMER
AND THE DOGS

During a severe winter, a Farmer found himself snowbound in his house. Sharply pressed for food, he began to eat his sheep. As the winter continued, he was forced to eat the goats also, and then the oxen. At this point, the Dogs said to each other, "Let's get out of here. If the master has no pity for the oxen, how likely is it that he will spare us?"

When our neighbor's house is on fire, it is best to look to our own.

THE HUNTER
AND THE WOODMAN

A Hunter, not very bold, was looking for the tracks of a Lion. He asked a Woodman felling oaks in the forest if he had seen any signs of the Lion's footsteps or if he knew where the beast's lair was. "If you come with me," said the Woodman, "I will show you the Lion himself." The Hunter, turning pale and chattering his teeth, replied, "No, thank you. It is only his track, not the Lion himself, I am in search of."

A hero is brave in deeds as well as words.

MERCURY AND THE SCULPTOR

Mercury, wanting to know how men viewed him, disguised himself as a traveller. Entering a Sculptor's workshop, he began asking the prices of the different statues he saw there. Pointing to an image of Jupiter, he asked how much the Sculptor wanted for it. "A drachma," he replied. Laughing to himself at the low price, Mercury asked about a figure of Juno, and the man mentioned a slightly higher price. Spying his own image, Mercury said, "You probably want more for this one?" "Well," said the Sculptor, "if you give me my price for the other two, I'll throw that one in for nothing."

Those who are anxious to know how the world values them will seldom be happy with the price.

THE MILLER, HIS SON,
AND THEIR ASS

A Miller and his Son were driving their Ass to a neighboring fair to sell the beast. They had not gone far when they met a troop of women collected round a well, talking and laughing. "Look there," cried one. "Did you ever see such fools, trudging along the road on foot when they could be riding?" Hearing this, the old man quickly told his Son to get on the Ass and walked along merrily by the beast's side. Presently they came near a group of old men in earnest debate. "There," said one of them, "it proves what I was saying. What respect is shown to old age in these days? Do you see that idle young rogue riding while his old father has

to walk? Get down, you rascal, and let the old man rest his weary limbs!" Upon this the old man made his Son dismount and got up himself. They had not proceeded far when they met a company of women and children. "Why, you lazy old fellow," cried several people at once. "How can you ride upon the beast while that poor little lad can hardly keep up by your side?" The good-natured Miller immediately had his Son join him on the Ass. They had now almost reached the town.

"Pray, honest friend," said a townsman, "is that Ass your own?" "Yes," said the old man. "Oh, I wouldn't have thought so," said the other, "by the way you load him. Why, you two fellows are better able to carry the

poor beast than he you." "Anything to please you," said the old man, "so let's try." The Miller and his Son tied the legs of the Ass together and, with the help of a pole, carried him on their shoulders over the bridge that led to town. This entertaining sight brought out crowds of people, till the Ass, not liking the noise or the situation, broke the cords that bound him and, tumbling off the pole, fell into the river. Upon this, the old Miller, vexed and ashamed, made his way home again, convinced that, by trying to please everyone, he had pleased nobody and lost his Ass, as well.

INDEX TO MORALS